The
Seven
Last Words
Of
Jesus Christ

Messages for Good Friday

Maurice A. Fetty

CSS Publishing Company, Inc., Lima, Ohio

THE SEVEN LAST WORDS OF JESUS CHRIST

Copyright © 2001 by
CSS Publishing Company, Inc.
Lima, Ohio

Scripture quotations are from the *Revised Standard Version of the Bible*, copyrighted 1946, 1952 ©, 1971, 1973, by the Division of Christian Education of the National Council of the Churches of Christ in the USA. Used by permission.

Some scripture quotations are from the *King James Version of the Bible*, in the public domain.

For more information about CSS Publishing Company resources, visit our website at www.csspub.com.

ISBN 0-7880-1787-X   PRINTED IN U.S.A.

Dedicated to
the loving memory of

Amanda Smith Quast
Mother of my late wife
Jane Smith Fetty

and to
the loving memory of

Melvin and Irene Lagerval
Parents of my wife
Sara Lagervall Fetty

in gratitude for their
steadfast faith, hope, and love.

Table Of Contents

Preface

The "Seven Last Words" of Jesus from the cross have entered indelibly into the Christian conscience. Every Good Friday, these words of pathos, anguish, and faith penetrate deeply into the heart of every person who has struggled with evil, forsakenness, and death.

In a time when many would prefer to bypass Good Friday by jumping from Palm Sunday to Easter, Jesus' final utterances from the Cross draw us inevitably toward the necessity of self-denial and total allegiance toward God. Son though he was, Jesus learned obedience through suffering, says the writer of Hebrews (5:8-9). And very often, so must we.

At some time in our lives, most of us will identify with the pathos of these words and thus find faith and courage in Jesus' noble example.

The First Word

"Father, Forgive Them"

*And Jesus said, "Father, forgive them; for they
know not what they do." And they cast lots to
divide his garments."*   — Luke 23:34

It was May 13, 1981. Even though accustomed to tragedy and
hardened to bloodshed, the world was shocked by what it saw on
its television screens and newspapers. There he was, bedecked in
his white robes, riding in his white jeep in St. Peter's Square, wav-
ing to the admiring crowds, when suddenly he fell backwards, grimacing in acute pain from an assassin's bullet.

In an instant, this much beloved peacemaker of the world, so
vigorous, so energetic, so persistent in his efforts of love and rec-
onciliation — in an instant Pope John Paul II's life hung in the
balance as he was rushed to the hospital.

Nearly two years later at Christmas of 1983, the world was
startled again, not by a peacemaking pope grimacing in pain from
the assassin's bullet, but by, of all things, a peacemaking pope
making peace with his would-be assassin. The media once again
flashed the picture around the world. There he was, Pope John Paul
II, in the prison cell in Rome, talking to Ali Agca, forgiving him of
the attempt on his life.

The zealous fanaticism was gone from the assassin's eyes as
the Pope held the very hand that held the gun which shot him.
Tender and loving words were exchanged. Ali Agca appeared to
kiss the Pope's ring and bow in a Muslim gesture of respect. Such
was the power of forgiveness.

I.

Flash back now about nineteen centuries to another white-
robed peacemaker much beloved by many, feared by others. He
was not assassinated by a fanatic. Instead, he was executed by the

establishment because they feared *he* was a fanatic, a troublemaker, a disturber of the peace.

It was better that one man perish than a whole nation be lost in revolution and counter-revolution, they said. And so they crucified him among the malefactors. But in his dying breath he was able to utter the almost impossible words, "Father, forgive them, for they know not what they do."

In our cynical mood, we are not too sure we really believe Jesus or his latter day servant, Pope John Paul. Did not, we ask, most assassins and executioners know exactly what they were doing? Did not John Wilkes Booth know what he was doing when he aimed the gun at Abraham Lincoln? Did not Lee Harvey Oswald know what he was doing when he murdered John Kennedy, or Sirhan Sirhan when he shot Robert Kennedy, or James Earl Ray when he took aim at Martin Luther King, Jr., or Arthur Bremer when he shot George Wallace, or John Hinckley when he put a bullet in President Reagan?

Most knew exactly what they were doing. In the name of a larger cause, in the authority of an alien power, in the fanatic vision of an altered world, they perpetrated their deeds of violence. But in the larger sense, they were desperate men of a desperate world, attempting to glorify self or a cause, to bring in a paradise of their own dreaming and their own devising.

It was the genius of Jesus to see the futility of those efforts for himself and for all men. Even *his* glorious vision and dream for a restored Davidic Kingdom or the arrival of the Messianic Age was not enough to induce him to lead yet another war to regain a lost paradise. "Father, forgive them, for they really do not know the vanity of what they do."

II.

However, on this tragic day, let us not be sentimental. Forgiveness does not mean an absence of judgment or justice. Jesus never said, "It's okay, go right ahead and pound in the nails. I forgive you." He never suggested they were right. The contrary. Like all acts of forgiveness, his implied judgment of the wrong. When Pope

John Paul went to Rebibbia Prison to forgive, he did not suggest release of the prisoner. Judgment, justice, and punishment remained.

When Jesus forgave, he did not call the wrong right. Instead he forgave the wrong in order to make things right with the wrongdoer. Theologian Paul Tillich reminds us that modern psychological insight and understanding do not replace judgment, nor should they undercut our courage to call wrong wrong (*The New Being*, p. 5).

Catholic theologian Robert Friday says, "Forgiveness doesn't mean that you become some sort of wimp and forgive without some kind of demand. We are responsible for what we have done" (*Time*, 1-9-84; p. 29). To accept the forgiveness is also to accept the judgment. It is to acknowledge guilt. As theologian Daniel Day Williams says, "Where there is no guilt, forgiveness is meaningless" (*The Minister And The Care of Souls*, p. 78).

Therefore, on this tragic day of execution of the Prince of Peace, it is fruitless to avoid blame and guilt by placing the blame on first century Jews and Romans. The judgment comes upon all of us in our grand schemes for a personal paradise to the exclusion of the brother in need. The judgment comes upon all of us in our conceit and arrogance and pride which arise out of our deep inward dread of insignificance and mortality. The judgment rests upon all who attempt to bring in the Kingdom of God by ungodly methods. And it is in the awakening of guilt, in the acceptance of responsibility for evil, in the acknowledgement of our deceit and mean-spiritedness that we are forgiven. Father, forgive them even more because they know now what they have done.

III.

Let us draw closer still. Let us come away from nations and peoples, from dread personal enemies, into our very homes and families and marriages. There is a sense today in which a man's enemies are those of his very household: female against male, child against parents, husband against wife. Some families are little more than polite armed camps where the grievances and grudges of years are hurled like stones at the slightest provocation. We blame, accuse, threaten, cajole, and take our revenge. Children blame parents for

11

an imperfect childhood. Parents blame children for a stressful life. Wives blame husbands for insensitivity and husbands blame wives for exploitation. Is this not the day to plead with our loving Creator, "Father, forgive us, for we both *do* and *do not* know what we do. We are caught in the dreadful circle of an eye for an eye, a tooth for a tooth"?

If, on this day, we can accept the judgment upon ourselves and others, we will be released from bondage to the hatreds of the past. We will be liberated from needing our enemy to establish our identity. We will be freed up from control by our enemy and the endless cycle of revenge upon revenge, reprisal upon reprisal, death upon death.

Thus this black Friday is Good Friday because God himself has judged *and* forgiven, not that the world should be condemned, but that it should be saved and made whole. God accepts us, loves us, forgives us, and asks us to do that with each other and thus release the power of change in the world. And if, on this day, we can do no other, perhaps we can at least do it in our families. "Father, forgive them and us, both when we do and do not know what we do." Amen.

The Second Word

"Today Shalt Thou Be With Me In Paradise"

And he said, "Jesus, remember me when you come into your kingdom." And he said to him, "Truly, I say to you, today you will be with me in Paradise." — Luke 23:42-43

Paradise is hard to come by these days. But then again, paradise has always been hard to come by. In fact, the majority of the world's people probably have never known anything closely resembling a lasting, enduring paradise. If we Americans, enjoying the highest standard of living ever known, have difficulty finding and keeping our private paradises, the world's teeming millions, often deep in poverty, frequently malnourished, regularly abused and exploited, might think of paradise as an ever-elusive dream.

The great population upheavals and migrations of the past might be understood in part as a search for paradise. There has forever been the longing for the fairer land, the better opportunity, the richer reward, and greater return for our labors. In search not only of religious freedom but economic opportunity as well, our Pilgrim fathers and mothers were determined to be a city set upon a hill, a light to all the nations. For them, America was the new Promised Land, the people of God with a Manifest Destiny to rise above the corruption and decay of the Old World to build a New World of righteous empire. For many, America was a new Garden of Eden where mankind, free from the evil of the past, would create a new age of justice, peace, and prosperity, based, of course, on holiness.

It mattered little to us that both the Bible and Milton had set forth in classic language and poetry the fact that paradise had been lost. Like migratory peoples of old in search of the golden age and the fountain of youth, we were confident paradise could be regained.

But at long last, America's age of innocence has passed. And it was a difficult passing, our fall from childhood into adolescent

13

wondering and adult guilt. But after slavery and a Civil War, after two World Wars, a Great Depression and several recessions, after assassinations and Korea and Cambodia and Vietnam, our age of innocence has gone forever, and with it, the elusive dream of paradise within this great republic. This is not to say we do not love this great land, nor is it to say we would trade it for another. It is only to say we have come of age.

I.

Our dreams were not unlike those of the thieves on the cross, and, for that matter, not unlike those of Jesus. If ever there were a prevailing notion among Jesus' contemporaries, it was that of the Kingdom of God, of a rule and reign paradisiacal in nature, when peace and prosperity, justice and righteousness would return to Israel. The Kingdom of God was a central theme of Jesus' teaching and preaching. And he found a ready audience in an expectant populace.

But if on the cross Jesus was committing his will to the will of God in the final act of submission and obedience, the brigands or malefactors crucified with him were continuing to assert their own will and dreams for the paradisiacal Kingdom — save for one.

Perhaps a part of the Zealot group devoted to military-political victory at any cost so as to establish their own version of paradise, these brigands were being crucified for what they truly were — that is, threats to Rome's paradisiacal self-image with Rome at the top and the rest of the world on the bottom. If Jesus had surrendered his vision of the Kingdom utopia to the larger will of God, these political brigands had not. Perhaps the equivalent of first century terrorists, they were committed to establishing their version of paradise.

The promise for political utopias continues. If Lenin and Marx incited revolution for a kingdom here and now, the beleaguered masses under Communist power wondered when they would have their share of the Kingdom. If capitalist countries pride themselves on an ever-higher standard of living, paradise is still elusive for millions where the rich tend to get richer and the poor, poorer.

And if economic systems never quite can deliver on paradise, political-economic solutions never quite make it happen either. New studies show that Lyndon Johnson's War on Poverty was at best a skirmish. The lot of the poor actually declined rather than improved, whereas the bureaucratic empire profited and grew.

II.

Ah, paradise, how elusive it is, even when we turn from political-economic agendas with a firm resolve to build a private paradise of our own making. If John F. Kennedy's Camelot came to a brutal, bloody end with an assassin's bullet, so too our private paradises seem short-lived. Were our high school years glorious? Did we peak instead at college with maximum freedom coupled with minimal responsibility and maximum stimulation? Did we finally get the kids through college and the parents well provided for only to discover how few are our years of enjoyment relatively free of heavy responsibility and economic burden?

Good Friday is good medicine for us all — extremely strong medicine, distasteful and irksome, but good medicine, nevertheless. It stands forever as a judgment upon false pride, upon naivete and arrogance. It is God's judgment upon the pretensions of all human efforts to regain paradise on our own terms. It is a reminder of the ultimate futility of all economic and political and religious systems which promise more than they can deliver. It is a revelation of the stark truth that

> *The worldly hope men set their hearts upon*
> *Turns ashes — or it prospers; and anon*
> *Like snow upon the desert's dusty face,*
> *Lighting a little hour or two — is gone.*

— Edward Fitzgerald, *The Rubaiyat of Omar Khayyam*

Alas, and so it was that the musical genius Mozart, so short-lived at only 35 years, was irreverently thrown into a pauper's grave. How fleeting even the Viennese paradise of musical genius.

But on the cross, the one thief now begins to see as Jesus has seen. Paradise is not an achievement of man, it is a gift of God. If

15

the first Adam in the Garden of Eden turned away from God to build his own paradise which ended in death, the new Adam, Jesus, now turns toward God to receive paradise back again as a gift of grace, responsive to faith.

And the thief sees what all the poor should see, that the paradisiacal Kingdom is not achievable, only receivable. If the simplicities of Sociology 101 assert that most crime arises out of poverty, the profundity of Good Friday is that paradise is not attainable by either rich or poor. The real paradise, the promise of life everlasting, is a gift of God given to those who lose their lives (that is, their private paradises) in order to gain them in the real paradise of God.

The one brigand died with the old, self-made vision of his private paradise. Today, our prayer should be that of the repentant brigand who saw the greater truth and requested paradise from him who was really able to give it. May we have that same wisdom, to hear Jesus' reassuring words, "Today, you will be with me in paradise."

The Third Word

"Woman, Behold Thy Son; Behold Thy Mother"

... [Jesus] said to his mother, "Woman, behold, your son!" Then he said to the disciple, "Behold, your mother!" And from that hour the disciple took her to his own home.

— John 19:26-27

Ask most sons and they will tell you their mothers do not understand them. How many mothers have their sons share deeply their thoughts and fears, dreams and aspirations? Sons, in their childhood, may talk to their mothers. But in their adolescence, youth and young manhood, they often seek out the company of other older women in whom they confide, and with whom they share their questions, their hopes, and dreams.

But ask most mothers if they understand their sons and they will claim they do. They will tell you their physical characteristics and personality traits from earliest infancy. They remember the first steps, the first word, the first time they slept through the night. Mothers can recall the excitement of a son over his first bicycle and the first day he really combed his hair and worried about how he looked to the girls.

Do mothers understand their sons? Ask them and they will recall a son's first date, his struggle with Latin and trigonometry, and his ego swelling after a series of victorious touchdowns. They will tell you how messy his room is, how unfortunate it is the son has inherited some of the personality flaws of his father. And when the son brings home some beautiful, young thing from college, the mother still holds herself superior in understanding. That young girl who claims to love him and to understand him really does not know him as does Mother. She could tell the girl a thing or two about her boy, good and bad. She knows her son better than anyone.

But does she really? Did Thomas Edison's mother understand him? Or Albert Einstein's mother? Did they really fathom what was going on inside them? Could Thomas Jefferson's mother say she really knew Tom better than he knew himself? Or Abraham Lincoln — could his mother claim to know what was going on in his mind and soul?

I.

Mothers often are bound by the old way of seeing, the customary way of thinking. They tend to define reality by what they have experienced rather than by the visions of their sons. They are likely to place their faith in what they have known to be true rather than in what their sons *hope* will become true.

Traditionally, mothers have clung to the old, producing and craving security, avoiding family-destroying risks. If mothers would have had their way, we probably would have had fewer martyrs, but we also would surely have had less progress. There comes a time when sons move beyond the understanding of mothers, attempting to make real a new idea, a new age, a new way the mothers might only have glimpsed dimly.

Thus Jesus the visionary, the prophet, the preacher-teacher and healer; Jesus the would-be revolutionary leader, the longed-for Khomeni-type Jewish Messiah who would set up a Jewish theocratic state like that of King David — this Jesus advanced beyond the understanding of his mother. Early in his public ministry, she and Jesus' brothers tried to get him to come home to the quiet carpentry business. Jesus' brothers mocked him and thought he was a little out of his mind. And maybe he was. For now, like other would-be Messiahs the Romans had executed, Jesus was himself being put to death for his visions and dreams.

Had it been worth it? Had it been a mistake to forsake his role as elder brother of a family of seven children, the role of chief provider after Joseph's death, to take up his mission for the Kingdom of God? Earlier in his ministry when his family came to take him home, he asked, "Who is my mother? Who are my brothers and sisters? They are those who share with me the vision of the Kingdom of God and have risked their lives in its behalf." Thus he identified himself with his cause, his new order, his new community more than with his genetic family.

II.

Many men and women have forsaken father, mother, and family for far less than the kingdom of God. Some pursue success around the world and only think of Mother at Christmas and birthday. Some tuck Mother away in a nursing home and neglect her completely as they pursue their pleasure. Others strive in behalf of career, notoriety, and materialistic reward to the neglect of honoring their parents.

Jesus had pursued the Kingdom of God despite the misgivings and misunderstanding of his mother. His brothers had not believed him. They had ridiculed and scorned him. Thus Jesus could not, in his hour of death, commend his mother to the security of his genetic brothers, who, after all, were *not* at the cross. They had not yet caught the new vision of the new order, the new day, the new age for which Jesus and his disciples labored and prayed.

Instead, he commended his mother to the care of John, his first cousin and beloved disciple, who *was* at the cross. John had left his fishing business with his father Zebedee for the sake of the Cause. Unlike Jesus' brothers, John had caught the vision of the new age and had risked his life for it and was the only disciple who was at the cross in the bitter end.

III.

Thus Mary's true security, her revered memory, was not kept so much by her genetic family, as it was by the church, the family of the faithful, the community of the new age. By entrusting Mary to John, the disciple, Jesus caused Mary to be remembered and revered beyond her wildest dreams and dearest imaginings.

Did Mary understand her son? Not really, not at the time of the cross. She thought this was the end. But understand him or not, she did understand this much: She loved him and in his hour of death, she knew he needed her, and she knew she needed to be with him. Despite misunderstandings, despite any feeling of recrimination she might have had about his foolish hopes, she *was* there, at the

19

foot of the cross saying, "I love you; I stand beside you in your hour of deepest loneliness." And it is noteworthy that, according to John's Gospel, there were four women at the cross, but only one man. Thus Saint Chrysostom observed centuries ago, "The weaker sex then appeared the more manly, so entirely henceforth were all things transformed."

And in his final moments, despite his disappointment in his mother's failure to understand, despite his identification more with the women who shared his vision of the new age than with Mary, despite his anguish at having a mother who did not really grasp what he was attempting to do in the world — despite all that, he loved her, and commended her to the care of John and thus of the church.

Regardless of the tragedy of this day, this black Friday of 29 or 30 A.D., love had its triumph. The evil which for a moment held the upper hand, now itself has been given the death blow, so much so that we call this *Good* Friday. And with new confidence mothers can give their sons to the cause of the new age, and sons can commend their mothers to fellow disciples, to the love and care of the church.

"Woman, behold thy son! Behold thy mother!"

The Fourth Word

"My God, My God, Why Hast Thou Forsaken Me?"

And when the sixth hour had come, there was darkness over the whole land until the ninth hour. And at the ninth hour Jesus cried with a loud voice, "E lo-i, E lo-i, la ma sabach-tha ni?" which means, "My God, my God, why hast thou forsaken me?" — Mark 15:33-34

Few of us have to be told what it means to be forsaken. Whether as a child we were lost from our mother, or as a youngster we were forsaken by our friends who ran off to hide and not play with us, or as a married person we were hurt by our partner's infidelity or devastated in his/her desire for a divorce, we know what it is to be forsaken. Even now many of us live in a lonely world, not really understood by anyone, and so alone we are quite sure it would make no difference to anyone if we lived or died.

Perhaps that is why Jesus' shriek on the cross holds such fascination for us. You would have thought the Gospel writers would have omitted it. After all, why would we want the one we later called Lord and Christ and Son of God to admit feeling forsaken by God? If he was the one who Christians later claimed brought them close to God, why would they preserve the very words which seemed to indicate Jesus himself was apart from God, alone and forsaken? We would tend to agree with Jesus' tormentors. If he was God's Son, why didn't God rescue him, bring him down from the cross, and exhibit a little power and glory to put the mockers and scoffers in their place.

I.

Strange and paradoxical though it may seem, Jesus had to practice what he preached. The deep truths he had shared with others

21

he now had to exemplify in his own life. He too had to deny his life to save it. In order to maintain his integrity, in order to be authentic, he had to submit himself to the will of God, even if it meant forsakenness and death. All his mighty teachings which held crowds spellbound seemed to fade away. All his great sermons which had inspired and challenged and rebuked now receded into the numbing pain of death. All his mighty acts of healing and the casting out of demons now seemed powerless to rescue him from this terrible inward silence, this agony of aloneness, this deep, dark void of the unknown.

His dreams of the coming kingdom evaporated in the high noon sun upon his bleeding brow. His visions of tender days in the peaceable kingdom were cut through with throbbing pain from pierced hands and side and feet. His mighty confidence in God's readiness to bring in the new age through his agency now waned as rapidly as his physical strength which flowed out of his body in sweat and blood and tears. "My God, my God, why hast thou forsaken me?" was no divine acting. It was the death cry of a forsaken man.

II.

Can any good come out of forsakenness? Is there any positive aspect to loneliness and weakness and reversal and humiliation and mockery? To what purpose might suffering and desolation be turned?

Forsakenness can have the positive effect of shattering our smugness and self-righteousness. It can remind us of how fragile and frail we are and can point out how we insulate ourselves with our riches, our intellectual concepts, our stuffy defensiveness, our inane habits, our obnoxious self-centeredness. In truth, we must, in many ways, die to come alive. Alas, even though terribly painful, it is often only through a "crucifixion" that we let go our suffocating self-concepts and stultifying habits of behavior, to be in touch with a larger and more exhilarating reality. God is not capricious, but he is thorough, and often allows our souls to undergo such ordeals as will cleanse us of pride and make us ready for the righteousness which is his gift.

How else could we call this Good Friday? For only in retrospect do we see that God's forsaking of Jesus was his final test. Unlike the first Adam of the Garden of Eden who grasped the world to himself and presumed to make himself immortal through the building of his own kingdom, this Jesus, the second Adam, the new man, surrendered his self-sufficiency, his dreams of messianic glory, for the sake of obedience to God. But in that surrender, he opened himself to God's larger reality. In his willingness to let go the temporal kingdom almost within his grasp, he later is given the eternal kingdom, which was both beyond his dreams and his grasp.

But God played for keeps and would allow no palliatives, no cushions, no escape routes, no sugarcoated bitter pill. Instead, Jesus underwent death in all its forms in utter nakedness and forsakenness. And so must we, for we must all die alone.

III.

But then comes Easter, that glad sunrise of the new day, the dawning of the new age, when our souls are caught up in new dreams and visions and realities heretofore unseen. And then, in the power of God, Jesus becomes Lord and Christ and inherits the kingdom eternal as Prince and Lord of all. And following him we enter into his great inheritance.

But it is by way of the cross, through the agony of forsakenness, through the severe demands of self-denial, through the terrible realization that all flesh is as grass. Yet, after the cross comes the crown; after the despair, the shout of triumph. Thus it is not black Friday, but Good Friday, and we are here for hope through all our forsakenness, because of Jesus, the pioneer and trailblazer of our faith.

The Fifth Word

"I Thirst"

After this Jesus, knowing that all was now finished, said (to fulfill the scripture), "I thirst."
— John 19:28

The surface of the earth is two-thirds water, but when you are really thirsty, a good drink can be hard to find. The human body is two-thirds water or more, but salty seas, brackish backwaters, contaminated ground water, and polluted lakes and rivers that catch on fire are not much comfort for a thirsty people. There is little that is more basic to life than water, and when you need it, it may be a matter of life and death.

It was, of course, for Jesus, a matter of death. In the hot agony of the crucifixion, the cool, fresh waves of the Sea of Galilee may have flashed through his mind. In the wrenching pain of nails and thorns, how refreshing might have been a drink from Jacob's well and how soothing a cool, wet towel across his bloody brow. If only the Samaritan woman were at hand to give him a drink as before.

It's not a pretty scene, this would-be Messiah dying of thirst. Somehow it doesn't seem to fit. The would-be deliverer and savior of his people, writhing in pain, with water, water everywhere, and not a drop to drink. How is it that the Son of God can be so frail, so helpless, and well, so human?

I.

But John wants us to know that we are not dealing with a phantom when we think of Jesus. Unlike the Gnostics who thought the Divine could not really be identified with a human body, John asserts from the beginning of his Gospel that in Jesus, "The Word became flesh and dwelt among us" (1:14). Unlike the Docetists who said it only seemed as though Christ was in the body of Jesus, and who affirmed that it only seemed as though Christ experienced

25

hunger and thirst, John asserts that God so loved the world, the material, physical, fleshly, bodily world, that he gave his Son in human life and suffering and death that the world might be saved.

In this simple but universal cry, "I thirst," John shows us that Jesus is one of us. Human life is not a mistake. Human bodies are not the creation of a lesser god. Our material hungers and thirsts are not illegitimate or somehow irreligious or beneath the dignity of the divine. Indeed, had not Jesus himself said, "Blessed is he who gives a cup of cold water in my name." And did he not depict the blessed in the last judgment as those who saw him naked and clothed him, hungry and gave him food, thirsty and gave him drink. With even his closest disciples gone, it was now a Roman soldier who, in an act of mercy, gave him to drink refreshing vinegar mixed with water and egg. Water, water everywhere, and the all-too-human Jesus needed it, and couldn't get it.

II.

But there is a deeper thirst than the physical. The Samaritan woman at Jacob's well knew that when she said, "Give me the living water of which you speak so that I may never thirst again." His disciples had known that when so many were forsaking him, but they had said, "To whom shall we go, for you have the words of eternal life." But now, at the crucifixion, they were not so sure. And at times, neither are we.

In his famous Sermon on the Mount, Jesus had said, "Blessed are those who hunger and thirst for righteousness, for they shall be satisfied." And John's Gospel records Jesus as saying, "If anyone thirst, let him come to me and drink. He who believes in me, as the scripture has said, 'Out of his heart shall flow rivers of living water' " (7:37-38).

It is the strange irony of the crucifixion that the very person who promised satisfaction in our longing for justice and righteousness is himself the victim of a gross miscarriage of justice. The one who suggested that he might be the source of living waters for the soul against the evils of the world, is now himself famished in body and soul at the hands of evil.

It was this contradiction which caused the disciples to forsake him. So long oppressed by foreign powers, so long beset by evil in its many forms, the disciples had believed again the promises of God that righteousness would prevail. Now they are not so sure, and neither are we. And could Jesus himself have been crying out for more than physical water? Was his not the deeper cry for solace for the soul, a more agonizing longing for justice and righteousness to slake the thirst for meaning in suffering and tragedy and sorrow?

III.

John loves symbolism. And if he wants to symbolize Jesus' complete physical and spiritual identity with our human dilemma, he also symbolizes the solution to our tragic state. When after his death, the Roman soldier pierces his side, blood and water gush forth, possibly symbolizing two key sacraments of the church — baptism and communion. While Jesus identifies with us completely in his death, we later identify not only with his death, but also with his resurrection.

Justice does triumph after all. Righteousness does in fact win the day. The fleeing, forsaking disciples are in fact drawn back to him to affirm boldly that Jesus has been vindicated. A new humanity has been born. A new age has begun, and we enter it through the waters of baptism and are sustained in it by the food of immortality, the bread and wine of the Eucharist.

Our hunger and thirst have been satisfied, but not completely. We have the assurance that human life is not futile, that injustice and evil will not win the day, and that the soul famished for living water will not be disappointed.

Nevertheless, with Paul, we affirm that in the present life, "we hunger and thirst" and that we sometimes serve "in toil and hardship through many a sleepless night, in hunger and thirst ..." (1 Corinthians 4:11; 2 Corinthians 11:27). Victory over physical and spiritual thirst in the present life is only temporal. But because of Jesus Christ, because of his resurrection and exaltation, we heed his great invitation, "Let him who is thirsty come, let him who desires take the water of life without price" (Revelation 22:17).

27

The Sixth Word

"It Is Finished"

*When Jesus had received the vinegar, he said,
"It is finished"; and he bowed his head and
gave up his spirit.* — John 19:30

In the time of Jesus, Rome was a great power, but it was a brutal power. True, it had extended the *Pax Romana* throughout the Mediterranean world and beyond, but it kept the peace with its powerful, well-trained legions who could kill without mercy. Yes, Rome had built its aqueducts and stadiums, its palaces and shrines, its triumphal arches and extensive roads. It had done so, not as a passive power, but as an aggressive power — conquering the world and dominating it not only with laws, but with legions — legions beyond number with horses, chariots, swords, and spears sharpened against enemies on any front.

And Jesus' Palestine was one of those fronts. Taking control from the corrupt Hasmoneans in 63 B.C., the Romans imposed their soldiers, taxes, and governors on would-be freedom fighters of left or right. A few years before the crucifixion of Jesus, the Roman general, Varus, crucified 2,000 Jews who were agitating for freedom. And a few years after Jesus' death, the Romans killed 3,000 Jewish men, women, and children accused of insurrection and rebellion. Rome had power, all right, and it was a brutal power.

That is why the Roman governor, Pilate, could agree with Jesus' words from the cross, "It is finished." Washing his hands of this troublemaker, Pilate was glad to be done with this potential insurrectionist in the time-honored Roman way of execution — crucifixion. Jesus had been accused of blasphemy, a religious charge of no interest to Pilate's irreligion. Jesus had also been accused of threatening to destroy the Jerusalem Temple, which would have been a sign of massive insurrection and revolt. More than that, Jesus' enemies accused him of claiming to be the new "Emperor of the Jews."

Rome would most assuredly hold Pilate accountable with his life if Jesus succeeded in leading any kind of revolt that threatened the status quo. So he put a sign on the cross in Latin, Hebrew, and Greek, which named the reason for his execution. In full view on the public thoroughfare, all could see the helpless, writhing, dying body of one claiming to be the new Jewish emperor. Let it be known, Pilate was saying from brutal Rome's position of power, the pretensions of this would-be Jewish emperor are over. This man Jesus is history. *It is finished!*

I.

Ironically, most of Jesus' disciples probably agreed with Rome's Pilate. Because many of the disciples firmly believed just what Pilate suspected, namely that Jesus was to be the new Jewish King or Emperor. They had left all to follow him, sometimes quibbling over who would get the most important appointments in the new administration, sometimes arguing over position and prestige, and sometimes wondering if they had made the right decision to leave behind family, career, and business to join Jesus' campaign.

And now, frankly and strangely, they agreed with their enemy, Pilate, that *"It is finished."* All their dreams of victory and glory had evaporated. All their hopes for freedom and independence were smashed. All their grand schemes for shaping a new form of government were scrapped. A dead Messiah is no Messiah at all. Rome had won again. *It is finished.*

And now comes the strange part, and in some people's ears, the heretical part — Jesus may also have agreed with Pilate and his followers. He had longed for a new day, a new time, when the reign of God would take precedence over the reign of men. He had envisioned a new era of brotherhood and sharing, tranquility and prosperity. He had hoped that by his powerful ministry and influence, the brutality of Rome and all earthly kingdoms would indeed be broken and the Kingdom of God would become an earthly reality.

But now, as the blazing sun beat upon his burnished brow, and now as the world whirled dizzily before his bulging eyes, and now as he faded in and out of consciousness as increasingly his body slumped and pulled against the flesh-tearing nails — now he wondered, are they not correct, is it not finished?

His body was still covered with the dried spittle from the jeering mobs. The coagulated blood from the 39 lashes of the cat of nine tails served as scant armor for the taunts, the jeers, the mockery shouted at him as at so many idealists and reformers of the world.

In and out of consciousness, struggling for breath, grimacing with pain and overwhelmingly depressed in spirit, one can imagine Jesus shouting at heaven as he had earlier when he felt so forsaken. He shouted with a loud voice when he died, shouted at God, shouted at the brassy heavens as we all do when failure crushes us with reality's harsh and cynical blows. Is it finished? Are we finished?

II.

Strangely, all of us who ever have failed feel great affinity with Jesus. All of us who now are failing, or all of us who feel we have not and are not accomplishing our life goals or fulfilling our ideals or achieving our destiny — all of us who have known defeat and reversal, confrontation and disease; all of us who have felt overwhelmed with massive, demonic powers crushing our greatest aspirations and suffocating our most noble inspirations — all of us identify with this failing Jesus when he shouts and then sighs, *it is finished.*

But there is another side to it all — a side John's retrospective Gospel likes — the side called accomplishment. "It has been accomplished," he might have said, or "completed" or "fulfilled," which is to say, after the agonizing prayer in the Garden of Gethsemane he never compromised his loyalty or swerved from his true calling. If his ideals were true, if his vision was from God, if his vocation was divine, he would not betray his Cause which some day must succeed to a cause which someday must fail.

So for all of us struggling for a kinder, gentler America; and for all of us seeking justice for the impoverished and exploited; and for all of us looking for the day when swords will be beaten into plowshares and spears into pruning hooks; and for all of us dreaming of the day when our relationships especially in marriage and family will be full of peace and joy and exhilarating communication and growth — for all such persons we can say

31

that in the sacrificial death of Jesus "it has been accomplished." The noble martyr is now leading a new humanity over a billion strong, all of whom look forward to the day when they can say of God's grand scheme of things entire, *"It is finished."*

The Seventh Word

"Father, Into Thy Hands I Commend My Spirit"

Then Jesus, crying with a loud voice, said,
"Father, into thy hands I commit my spirit!"
And having said this he breathed his last.
— Luke 23:46

Perhaps no scene is more indelibly impressed in the conscious-ness of western civilization than that of Good Friday. No public execution has ever received more public notice. No so-called inci-dental death at the hands of the state has ever taken on more sig-nificance. And no last words of any death row criminal are better known than these seven last words of Jesus of Nazareth.

This last word from the cross, "Father, into thy hands I com-mend my spirit," was a nighttime prayer from Psalm 31:5, taught by every Jewish mother to her children. Only a few short years earlier, Mary had tucked the child Jesus into bed, listening ten-derly as he commended his spirit to the Heavenly Father's care during the threatening hours of darkness.

And now, at the end of his life at age 33, we might have ex-pected something different from the taunted, mocked, suffering prophet of Galilee. We might have expected cursing the God who seemed to forsake him. We might have expected derisive scorn for all the idealism of political and social reform he once espoused. We might have expected a caustic cynicism and rancid skepticism about the so-called justice of God. But instead, we get this night-time prayer he learned as a child, "Father, into thy hands I com-mend my spirit."

I.

Public words of public speakers often come back to haunt them. In his famous Sermon on the Mount spoken to thousands,

33

he blessed those who mourn, assuming they would find comfort, a comfort which seemed far removed from him now. He had told the thousands, "Blessed are you when men revile you and persecute you and say all manner of evil against you falsely for my sake. Rejoice, and be exceeding glad, for great is your reward in heaven." Those words must have been haunting him now as he writhed in unspeakable pain at the hands of his persecutors.

And his words to the multitudes of Palestine whom he saw as helpless, neglected sheep without a shepherd? He assured them they were of infinite worth in the eyes of God. Not a sparrow falls, but the Heavenly Father notices, he told them. Every hair of your head is numbered, so how could you feel God has forgotten you, he told the weary peasants.

But just earlier from the cross, the calming words of the Sermon on the Mount seemed to evaporate as he shrieked, *"E lo-i, E lo-i, la ma sabach-tha ni"* — "My God, my God, why hast thou forsaken me?" The earlier assurances of the powerful prophet of Nazareth seemed squeezed from every cell of his body. But yet he prayed his childhood nighttime prayer as the nighttime of death was about to overtake him, "Father, into thy hands I commend my spirit."

However, the scene and the mood were radically different from the peaceful childhood bedroom of Nazareth. Luke tells us that earlier in the Garden of Gethsemane, Jesus prayed so intensely, so agonizingly, that he sweat, as it were, great drops of blood. "Father, if it be thy will, let this cup of suffering pass from me."

Notice, the word is still "Father," not "fate" or "chance" or "brutal indifferent forces" or "vague cosmic force" or "energy of the universe." History is still very personal and God is still very personal, despite the impending mockery, humiliation, and brutal execution.

And now, in these last dying moments on the cross, the word is still "Father," and the utterance is still a prayer in place of curses. The passers-by railed against him, taunting him to save himself and them. The religious leaders, whom you would have expected to be sympathetic, mocked him, saying, "He saved others but cannot save himself. Come down from the cross that we may see and believe," they shouted.

But there were no curses from his mouth. There was no loathing contempt, no self-righteous condescension which sometimes accrues to the falsely accused. There was not even bitter resignation to the "fates." Instead, there was the prayer of faith, "Father, into thy hands I commend my spirit."

III.

Thus, in the end, what we have is what God was looking for from the beginning, namely a commendable spirit. If Adam and Eve rebelled in paradise, and if the rebellions and atrocities increased across the centuries in ungodly men and women, in Jesus, the completely obedient Son of God, we have then the reversal of history. In the heights of temptation and in the depths of approaching death, we have in Jesus a spirit commendable to God. In Jesus, we have the Son, who tasted death for everyone, maintaining a commendable spirit.

As Peter's first letter puts it, Jesus "committed no sin; no guile was found on his lips. When he was reviled, he did not revile in return; when he suffered, he did not threaten; but he trusted him who judges justly" (1 Peter 2:22-23). Hanging naked before the mob, the last gasps of breath shorter and shorter, the darkness rolling in and out of Jerusalem as his own mind struggled with the darkness of doubt and despair — hanging naked and alone, Jesus writhed in the crucible of history.

The surging multitudes once singing his praises cursed him now. The women once struggling to touch the hem of his garment to heal their hemorrhages were now revulsed by the blood coagulating on his distended body. And his fair, grand vision of the kingdom of God faded over the horizon of consciousness.

But in the end he did not curse or revile or threaten. Instead, he shouted in a loud voice, shouted his childhood prayer across the centuries, shouted his exemplary affirmation of faith for all who follow him into the worst death has to offer, shouted for all the ages from a commendable spirit, "Father, into thy hands I commend my spirit." And in our hour of death, he bids us pray as he prayed, without bitterness or cursing or reviling, praying loudly or softly, "Father, into thy hands I commend my spirit."